D1190028

Introducing...

... three little friends who want to be friends with you. If you let them, they'll take you on the most magical adventures you can imagine.

Who are they? Their names are Heada, Heartly and Doofer. They're all very different, because they come from three different lands in the wonderful Kingdom of Theysay.

This is Heada from The Land of Thinking. She wears big, green glasses and, like all the Thinkers, she's a whiz at thinking. Quick as a wink she can think up an answer, make up a rainy day game or find a hiding place.

This is Heartly from The Land of Feeling. He has long, floppy ears and soft, cuddly fur. Like everyone in his land, Heartly feels a million emotions. In a second, his feelings can change from sad to happy, or from scared to excited.

This is Doofer from The Land of Doing. He's always ready for action. He can build a birdhouse, hit a homerun or juggle three oranges in one hand! When he's busy (which is constantly!), he's a buzzing whirlwind with long, yellow hair flying in the breeze.

In the Kingdom of Theysay also lives a mysterious and magical man known as The Great Theysayer. His home is the Hall of Harmoniousness, which stands high on a majestic mountain.

They say The Great Theysayer is very wise. Over the years, he has learned the truths about all the "they says" that have ever been said.

One day he looked at the many books of "they says" in his library and remembered how long and hard he had worked to become so wise. Wouldn't it be wonderful, he thought, if children could learn more easily! But how?

Gradually a great plan took shape in his mind. He would choose one special person from each land in the Kingdom. He would send them on missions to help children learn some of life's most important lessons. By helping the children, they would also learn a lot themselves.

Can you guess who he picked for the missions? Heada, Heartly and Doofer! They were the very best at thinking, feeling and doing.

To help them, The Great Theysayer gave each a gift: a thick book called the Tome to Heada, a magic crystal to Heartly and an amazing bag to Doofer.

Heada's book was stuffed with all the things they would need to know for their missions. She always carried it in her kangaroo-like pouch.

When anyone held Heartly's crystal, it glowed different colors to show feelings—pink for happiness, gray for sadness, and so on through a whole rainbow of emotions.

And in Doofer's amazing bag could be found all kinds of wonderful and surprising things to help them on their way.

After receiving their gifts, Heada, Heartly and Doofer began their exciting adventures. This is the story of one adventure.

Library of Congress Catalog Number: 85-45422
ISBN:
0-934275-06-8
Published in the United States by Family Skills, Inc.
Manufactured in the United States of America

A Lasting Friend

Friendship: *Making Friends*

Authors
J. Thomas Morse, M.A.
Betty Gouge, Ph.D.
Deanna Tate, Ph.D.
John Eickmeyer

Research and Editing
Mary Thrash, M.A.
Teri Gathings, M.S.
Linda Stanislao, B.S.

Illustrations
Cathie Bleck

Published by Family Skills, Inc., Dallas, Texas.
Distributed by Kampmann & Company, Inc., New York, New York.

*Family Skills, Inc. wishes to acknowledge and express our sincere thanks
to the hundreds of children and parents who contributed to the research,
design, development and testing of the KidSkills™ interpersonal skills series.*

*I*t was early one morning at *The Hall of Harmoniousness. The newly risen sun shone brightly through the columns of the courtyard. The sunlight made rainbows in the splashing fountain. The birds twittered cheerfully and hopped through the dewy grass looking for their breakfasts.*

Inside the Hall, all was quiet. Everyone was still sleeping peacefully. Not a sound disturbed the dreamy hush, until ...

WHAM! WHAM! WHAM!

Heada and Heartly sat up in their beds.

"What was that?" Heada wondered aloud.

"I don't know!" Heartly gasped, his long ears quivering with startled surprise. "But it sure woke me up!" he grumbled.

WHAM! WHAM! WHAM! went the noise again.

"A peculiarly peculiar sound," observed Heada thoughtfully as she put on her green glasses. "I think we'd better find out what it is."

So Heada and Heartly jumped from their beds and scurried off to see what was going on.

In the Great Ceremonial Chamber, they found Doofer busily nailing boards together with a hammer.

"That looks like fun!" chirped Heartly gaily.

"What are you making?" Heada asked.

"I don't know," Doofer replied with a grin. "But it's going to be wonderful!" WHAM! WHAM! WHAM!

"May I see your plans?" asked Heada. She loved looking at diagrams.

"Never use 'em!" laughed Doofer. "In The Land of Doing where I come from, we just get started and hope for the best." WHAM!   WHAM!

Heada smiled and shook her head. "In The Land of Thinking where I'm from, my friends and I would study and study and study the plans and never get started at all!"

"My friends in The Land of Feeling would rather paint a picture of something than build it," said Heartly. "I miss my friends," he added sadly.

Heada looked thoughtful. "I think friends are to be missed when you are apart. Do you miss your friends, Doofer?"

"Yes!" yelled Doofer, struggling to lift a heavy plank, "especially when I'm ... PUFF! PUFF! PUFF! ... building!"

Heada and Heartly rushed to help him set the board in place. Then they held it steady as Doofer sawed off one end. The fresh smell of wood and sawdust filled the great room. Finally, he drove two nails through the board with loud bangs of his hammer.

"Finished!" he crowed and pointed proudly to the crooked jumble of boards and bent nails.

"But what have you made?" asked Heada as Heartly looked on curiously.

"I don't know, but I got you to help me." Then his two eyes gleamed slyly in his furry face. "Maybe I'll call it a helper finder!" he shouted triumphantly.

A gentle chuckle sounded behind them. The three turned around as The Great Theysayer himself entered the chamber.

"It's good to see you working so well together," he said, "because I have a new mission for you. And you'll get to help someone make something else."

"What?" asked the three eagerly.

"Something very important to everyone. You were speaking of it just now."

"Helpers?" asked Doofer, pointing at Heada and Heartly.

"Not exactly," said The Great Theysayer. With that, he disappeared behind one of the tall marble columns that supported the roof of The Great Ceremonial Chamber. When he returned, he was pushing a white cardboard box about three feet high. On one of the sides were printed the words "A New Friend."

"I understand!" said Heada, her eyes brightening. "Friends are what we were talking about. We're going to help someone learn how to make friends."

"Exactly!" said The Great Theysayer.

"But what's in the box?" asked Doofer as he examined the carton curiously.

"Something you'll need for this mission," said The Great Theysayer. "Something rather unusual," he added mysteriously. "But don't open it until you reach your destination. For now, you must wait and see!"

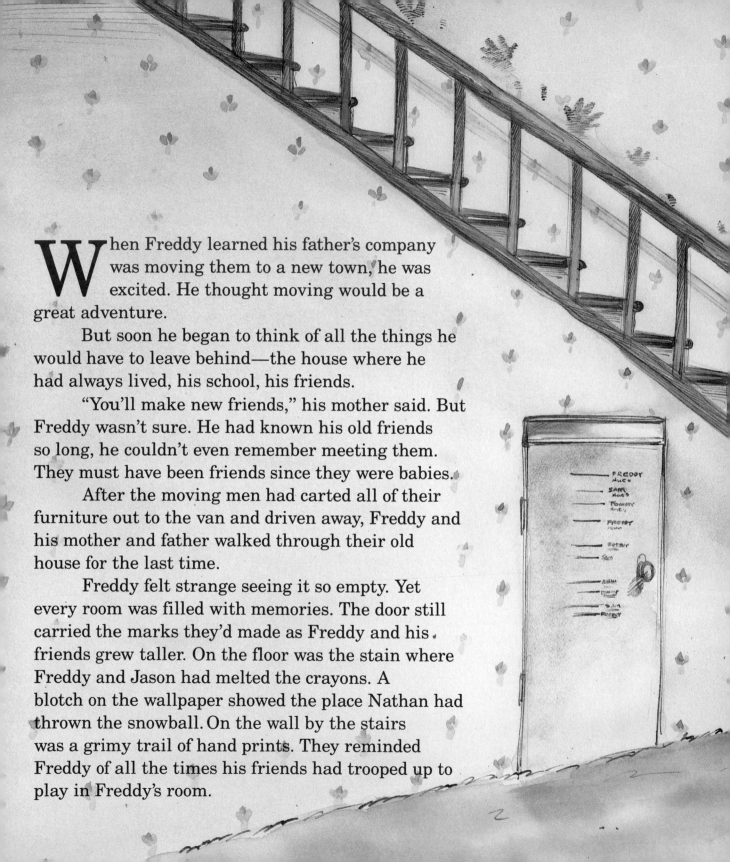

When Freddy learned his father's company was moving them to a new town, he was excited. He thought moving would be a great adventure.

But soon he began to think of all the things he would have to leave behind—the house where he had always lived, his school, his friends.

"You'll make new friends," his mother said. But Freddy wasn't sure. He had known his old friends so long, he couldn't even remember meeting them. They must have been friends since they were babies.

After the moving men had carted all of their furniture out to the van and driven away, Freddy and his mother and father walked through their old house for the last time.

Freddy felt strange seeing it so empty. Yet every room was filled with memories. The door still carried the marks they'd made as Freddy and his friends grew taller. On the floor was the stain where Freddy and Jason had melted the crayons. A blotch on the wallpaper showed the place Nathan had thrown the snowball. On the wall by the stairs was a grimy trail of hand prints. They reminded Freddy of all the times his friends had trooped up to play in Freddy's room.

Outside Freddy kicked at the summer grass
growing high in the yard, and an old baseball rolled
out from among the weeds. He picked it up and thought of all the ball games
he had played with his friends in the yard.

The sun beat down as Freddy's dad loaded the last suitcase into the car.
"Whew!" he said, mopping his brow. "Well, it's time to get going."

"Bye, Freddy!" called a trio of voices as Freddy pulled open the car
door. He turned to see three glum faces looking at him over the hedge that lined
the driveway.

Freddy dropped his head and felt a wave of sadness pass over him. The lump in his throat felt as big as the baseball he carried. Without saying a word, he lobbed the baseball over the hedge. Three pairs of hands reached for it, but Freddy didn't wait for the catch.

He turned and ran back to the car. As he climbed in the back seat, he swallowed hard to hold back the tears. And the next thing he knew, the old house and the old neighborhood were fading into the distance out the rear window. Three small figures ran across the yards, then vanished from Freddy's sight.

Suddenly, Freddy felt as empty as the house.

The drive seemed to take forever. Finally, Freddy's father said they were coming into the new neighborhood.

The neighborhood was nice enough. The houses stood among half-grown shade trees along broad, winding streets.

There were still a few vacant lots around where Freddy saw packs of kids playing baseball and other games. Everybody seemed to know everybody else. But Freddy knew no one.

In the days that followed, no one rang his doorbell on those long, hot afternoons.

Freddy remembered how his old friends were always coming over to play. Having friends had

seemed so easy and natural then, like waking up in the morning. He couldn't remember having done anything special to meet them. Didn't friends just "happen"? Wasn't friendship supposed to be like that?

Maybe not. At least, not here, Freddy thought. He felt lonely for the first time in his nine years. He felt angry, too—at the stupid company for moving them away—angry at Dad for agreeing to move. Why hadn't he said no?

He kept hoping he'd wake up and it would all be a bad dream. He'd be back home in Riverton with his pals. But each morning found him in the same unfamiliar bedroom with the same uneasy feeling. He seemed to forget his loneliness when he watched television.

"I wish you'd get outside more," said Mother one afternoon as Freddy sat slumped in front of the TV watching cartoons. "Why don't you go and find somebody to play with?"

"I don't have anybody," Freddy sulked.

"Then find somebody," Mother insisted.

"I don't know how," muttered Freddy under his breath, but he wasn't sure Mother heard.

"You won't make friends staring at a television," she continued, switching off the TV. "Now go on. Get some exercise. It's summer, and you're pale as a peeled potato."

"It's no fun playing by myself," said Freddy glumly. "And nobody around here wants to play with me."

"You haven't given anyone a chance," replied Mother. But then she saw the hurt look in Freddy's eyes.

"I don't know how to make friends," said Freddy simply.

Mother ruffled Freddy's brown hair. "I know it's hard sometimes," she said. "You had so many buddies back in Riverton. You'll make new friends — at least when school starts."

"School won't be for two months, and I might just lie here until then," Freddy groaned, flopping on his back.

"Ohhhh, no, young man. I want you out from under foot," said Mother, nudging him gently with her toe. "Outside, now. Go! Go!" She flapped her hands at Freddy, but he didn't move.

"Hmmmm," mused Mother to herself. This was more difficult than she had thought. She wandered to the window and gazed out.

"I wonder what's in those woods over there," she said casually.

"What woods?" asked Freddy, showing a glimmer of interest.

"Right over there," Mother replied, pointing out the back window. Freddy sat up and followed the line of her pointing finger with his eye.

There beyond the back fence was an inviting cluster of trees that crowned the top of a hill.

"Looks kind of interesting," suggested Mother quietly, watching Freddy's reaction.

"Yeah," he said softly, almost to himself. He got up and went to the window to get a better look. "Maybe I'll go see," he said, his eyes fixed on the cool looking shade beneath the tree branches. "Just for a little while."

The woods were murmuring with the hum of insects and the music of birds. Freddy followed a path among the tall trees.

He breathed deeply, smelling the rich, earthy odors of moss and mud and dead leaves. He felt a cool breeze on his cheek and heard the gurgling of water over stones nearby.

Freddy smiled. He was alone, but somehow in this special place, he didn't feel lonely.

A brilliant butterfly flashed its blue and gold wings before Freddy's eyes, and away he ran after it, jumping over fallen logs and running along broken pathways to follow its airy, floating dance.

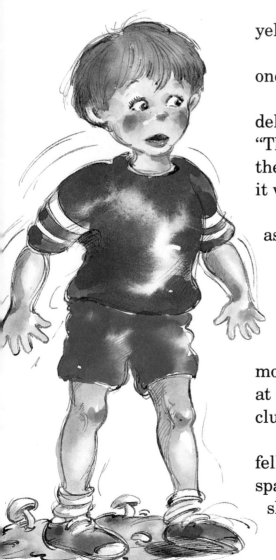

Suddenly, he saw something that made him stop. In the hollow trunk of a large tree was a white cardboard box. He picked up a short stick and gave the box a poke. It started moving!

Freddy jumped back a few steps as the box slid forward out of the tree. Behind it came three funny little characters who were pushing with all their might.

"PUSH! PUSH! PUSH!" commanded the hairy yellow one who seemed to be leading the team.

"I think there's an easier way," puffed the one with green glasses, "if I had time to think of it."

The one with big ears seemed to glow with delight. "It feels good to be outside again!" he gasped. "That was a tight squeeze!" He looked back inside the tree where an odd light shone for a moment. Then it went dark as though a door had closed.

Freddy's mouth dropped open in amazement as he listened. Were these little creatures really real?

The one with green glasses was peering curiously about as she dusted herself off. Suddenly, she caught sight of Freddy. "I think it's him!" she exclaimed.

The others turned and looked, and for a moment Freddy and the little threesome just stared at each other. Then they came bustling over and clustered around the boy.

"Let's be sure he's the right one," said the little fellow with big ears. And he brought out a big, sparkling crystal about the size of a baseball. It shimmered with a glowing pink light until he put it into Freddy's hands; then it turned deep blue.

"The lonely color," sighed big-ears. "That's the lonely color, all right."

Freddy was amazed. He stared at the crystal. It felt cool and smooth as he rolled it between his hands. And it glowed with the color of his own feeling? And the creatures? Were they real? Should he trust them? They seemed harmless— even quite friendly. Yet he felt so confused by it all!

"I've never seen lonely that blue," big-ears said. "You must be Freddy."

And with that the introductions began. Heada, Heartly and Doofer told Freddy their names and that they'd been sent by The Great Theysayer who knew all about Freddy's loneliness. He'd even given them something to help, though they weren't sure what it was. Freddy listened to their story with wide-eyed wonder, hardly saying a word.

"And so," concluded Heada a few minutes later, "here we are, and here *you* are, and here's the box The Great Theysayer sent."

"Let's open it!" shouted Doofer eagerly. And reaching into the bag he carried, he pulled out a small pocketknife. "S-S-S-S-SNICKETY POP!" he said, extending a blade.

It was a moment's work to cut the tape that held the box closed. As Doofer pulled back the flaps, Freddy stared at the lettering on the box's side. "A New Friend" it said. He didn't know what to make of that. What could it mean?

"It's a mechanical man!" Doofer yelled, looking inside. "Or parts of one."

"More precisely, a robot," observed Heada.

"How exciting!" squealed Heartly.

"How do we put it together?" wondered Freddy as Doofer lifted out mechanical arms, legs, body and a head like a small TV set.

"The Tome may tell us!" Heada exclaimed. From the kangaroo-like pouch on her tummy, she withdrew a thick book and began flipping the pages. "Here it is: 'Robots, Friendly. Assembly and Operating Instructions.'"

While Heada read from the Tome and Heartly flapped his ears excitedly, Doofer and Freddy snapped the little robot together. When they were done, everyone looked for the ON switch, but none could be found.

"All the Tome says is: 'Make Friends,'" Heada reported as she closed the book.

"But how?" asked Freddy, peering into the robot's blank video screen face. "Hey!" he called. "Hey, Mr. Robot!" Nothing happened.

"I always feel friendlier when I know someone's name and they know mine," suggested Heartly.

Freddy hesitated. He felt a little silly talking to a machine, but he decided it was worth a try. So he cleared his throat and said quietly, "Ahem. My name's Freddy. Can you hear me?" Nothing happened.

He tried again, this time a little louder and more cheerfully. "My name's Freddy. What's yours?"

Suddenly, the robot began to hum, and rows of colored lights on its chest began to flicker. A mechanical-sounding voice said: "Hello, Freddy. My name is ALF."

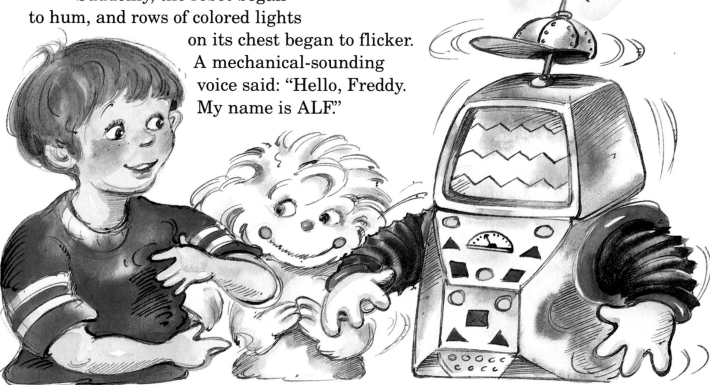

Everyone clapped excitedly at this success. But nothing else happened, and Freddy didn't know what to do next.

"I like to know more about people I meet before I think of them as friends," said Heada. "Tell him a fact about yourself."

Freddy thought for a moment, then said: "I'm nine years old. How old are you, ALF?"

ALF's video screen lit up. "I am one minute and seven seconds old," said the voice. But the face remained a blank square of light.

"I feel closer to someone when I know where they're from," mused Heartly.

Freddy turned to the robot. "I was born in Riverton, but I live near here now. Where are you from, ALF?"

"I was made in the workshop of The Great Theysayer, but I was assembled here," replied ALF. Patterns of color began to flow across his screen.

Next Doofer spoke up. "I like friends to *do* things with me. Ask him to play a game."

Freddy looked around for something to play a game with. Under a cluster of ferns he spied an old, discarded tennis ball.

"Would you like to play catch, ALF?" he asked as he brushed the dirt off the ball.

ALF held out his mechanical arms and clapped his hands three times. Freddy grinned and tossed the ball. ALF caught it neatly and tossed it back. The patterns of color on his screen became a smiling face. The two smiled happily at each other as they tossed the ball back and forth, back and forth.

"He's doing indescribably well," Heada whispered to Doofer. "He's really making a friend." Heartly felt so happy, he turned a cartwheel.

Suddenly, ALF made a bad toss, and the ball smacked Freddy in the forehead. "Ouch!" said the boy, rubbing the spot. "Ha, Ha, Ha," laughed ALF mechanically. There was a moment's pause. Then Freddy felt anger welling up inside of him. "Laugh at me, will ya?" he yelled, jumping up and stomping away.

He found the ball where it had rolled, picked it up and threw it back hard. It hit ALF in the rows of lights on his chest, and immediately his video screen face went dark. The humming stopped, too.

"Oh no!" wailed Freddy. "I've broken him!"

Everyone gathered around ALF and looked to see what would happen next. But the robot remained motionless and silent.

Heartly wrapped a long, comforting ear around Freddy's shoulders. "I'm sorry," he murmured sympathetically. "I'm sorry."

"I'm sorry, too," Freddy said. "I wish I hadn't gotten so mad. I wish I hadn't hit him."

"Perhaps you should talk to ALF," suggested Heada. "Isn't that what friends would do?"

"Wouldn't do any good," Freddy sighed. "He wouldn't listen."

"A friend would," Heada continued. "Listen to this." She pulled out the Tome and began to read. "A friend is someone who listens and talks to you. A friend understands and accepts you the way you are. Friends are honest and straightforward with each other. They share their feelings, especially when working out problems."

Heartly liked what he heard, and he spoke up in a singsong voice:

"A friend isn't someone who never *gets mad,*
Who never makes blunders or makes you feel
  sad.
But friends share their feelings and then
  make amends.
And that is the way that they always stay
  friends."

"Go on!" urged Doofer. "Talk to him! Tell him how you feel."

Freddy looked at ALF's blank face. "I'm sorry ALF," he began slowly. "I know you didn't mean to hit me with the ball." Nothing happened.

Freddy turned to the others with a helpless look, but they motioned for him to continue. "When you laughed at me," he went on, "I got mad. So I threw the ball back at you hard. Please don't be mad." Nothing happened.

Freddy took a deep breath and gave it one more try. "I wish I hadn't hit you, and I'm sorry, okay?"

One red light glowed on ALF's chest. "No more 'Ha! Ha!' No more 'Ha! Ha!'" the little mechanical voice said softly, then added, "Control yourself, control yourself, control yourself."

Freddy's face brightened with relief. "I will," he said. "Still friends?"

Suddenly, all of ALF's lights came on again brighter than ever. His video screen face lit up, but this time, instead of colors or a drawing, there was the image of a real boy's face grinning back at Freddy.

"Sure, Freddy," he said. His voice was no longer mechanical. "You're too good a friend to lose!"

"Wow!" breathed Freddy. "You're real!"

"Not exactly," smiled ALF. "But *you* are. And you know how to be a real friend. So get out there and make some friends, just like you did with me."

"But I don't need any other friends if I've got you, ALF," said Freddy. "Come home and stay with me."

"I can't," ALF replied. "I've got to go back to the kingdom of The Great Theysayer with Heada, Heartly and Doofer."

"Awwww," sighed Freddy in disappointment.

"It doesn't mean I don't like you," ALF added. "We'll still be friends. But I've got other jobs to do."

Freddy smiled in spite of himself. "Yeah. I guess a friend understands and accepts you the way you are, right?"

"Right!" grinned ALF. Then he looked up, listening. "Stand by for a message!" he said. And suddenly the picture changed as though someone had switched the channel. On the screen appeared the face of a wise old man with a long, silvery beard. Freddy stared spellbound at the kind, blue eyes beneath the twilight blue hood.

"The Great Theysayer!" whispered Heada, Heartly and Doofer together. Freddy couldn't believe his eyes!

The Great Theysayer spoke in his deep, gentle voice:
"Friends keep a permanent place in your heart,
But they say even good friends sometimes have to part.
Friends remain friends where ever they roam,
But they say even good friends must go home."

"And now it's time for you to come home!" he called. "This mission is accomplished!"

As the face faded from view, Freddy waved, wondering if The Great Theysayer could see him. And what did those words mean: "Mission accomplished"? Freddy wasn't sure.

Then ALF reappeared on the screen. "C'mon, team!" he said. "Let's get going." The little robot turned and led the way back to the hollow tree. Heada, Heartly and Doofer followed, stepping inside one after another. As the bright light came on from below, all of them waved to Freddy, and ALF gave him a wink. "So long, Freddy," he said just before they all sank out of sight.

As they disappeared, Freddy ran to the tree and shouted after them: "What does ALF mean?"

A fading voice replied, "A Lasting Friend!" Then the light vanished, and when Freddy looked inside the hollow trunk, all he saw was a thick carpet of moss and old pine needles.

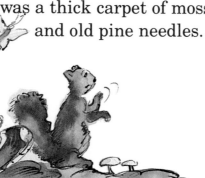

reddy walked slowly back along the path through the woods. He didn't hear the sounds or see the colors around him now. He was deep in thought.

His meeting with Heada, Heartly, Doofer and ALF had been fun and exciting. But who could he tell? Who would believe him? Not even his friends back home would accept such a wild tale.

At a turn in the path, Freddy nearly bumped into another boy coming from the opposite direction. They exchanged nods without speaking and stepped carefully around each other on the narrow path.

The stranger was about Freddy's age and size. He stopped for a minute and called over Freddy's head to someone behind him on the path: "C'mon, Michael! Hurry up!"

Freddy sighed and started to walk on. The lonely feeling was rushing back. "They've got each other for friends," he thought. "What would they want with me?"

But then he thought of ALF, and his mind began racing. Suddenly, he remembered something— something important. If he hadn't talked first, ALF would never have come to life. Freddy had worked to get ALF started. He'd introduced himself and asked questions. He'd shared some thoughts and feelings, and spent time to become friends.

Maybe real friends were like that, too. Maybe friendships didn't just "happen" after all. Maybe someone had to get them started.

As Freddy looked back at the boy, something about him seemed familiar. Finally, Freddy was brave enough to speak.

"Hi," he said. Surprised, the boy turned and looked at Freddy.

Freddy almost gave up right then, but he made himself continue. "My name's Freddy Lloyd," he said. "What's yours?"

The moment's pause seemed to last forever as Freddy waited for an answer. Then the boy smiled and came down the path.

"Alfred Jameson," he replied. "But you can call me Alf. Everyone does."

Freddy grinned broadly. Now he knew what he recognized about the boy. His face was the one from the video screen! Freddy felt as if he knew him already.

"We moved into that house over there last month," Freddy said, pointing in the direction of home. "You live around here, Alf?"

"Down at the end of the block," said Alf. "Where'd you move from, anyway?"

"Riverton," Freddy answered.

Alf's face brightened. "My grandmother lives in Riverton! I've been there lots of times. It's neat."

"Yeah," said Freddy. "I miss it."

A crashing noise in the bushes caught their attention. Suddenly, a boy sprang out upon them.

"Gotcha!" he yelled triumphantly as he saw their look of surprise.

Alf laughed. "Freddy, this is Michael."

Michael tossed his hair out of his eyes and looked at Freddy curiously. "Are you Freddy Lloyd?" he asked.

Freddy nodded.

"My dad works with your dad," Michael said. "He asked me about you. I've been looking for you. Where ya been?"

"Oh," smiled Freddy. "Here and there."

"A man of mystery!" said Michael with a twinkle in his eye. "That's what we need around here—more mystery and adventure!" He crouched down and stalked a few steps up the path, imaginary rifle at his side.

"We're going exploring," said Alf. "Want to come, Freddy?"

"Sure!" Freddy replied.

"Warn him about the tigers," called Michael.

Alf chuckled. "Yes!" he said, playing along. "You gotta be on the lookout all the time."

"I'm ready," Freddy said.

"C'mon, guys!" called Michael impatiently, waving for them to follow. "In this jungle, *anything* can happen!"

The three moved forward together into the shadows, darting looks this way and that, eyes narrowed to slits like hunters seeking their prey. "Careful of the tiger traps!" warned Alf as Freddy stumbled over a shallow dip in the path.

"Hey! Look at this!" cried Michael as they passed a big, hollow tree. There on the other side stood a large, white box. The top was open, and it was clearly empty. The boys gathered around and stared at it.

"Look at what it says," Alf exclaimed, pointing at the lettering on one side. "A New Friend," he read aloud.

Both he and Michael turned and looked at Freddy curiously. Then they began to laugh. "We've made new friends before," they roared. "But you're the first one that ever came in a box!"

A NEW FRIEND

With that remark, Freddy looked startled. Were they making fun of him? Freddy wasn't sure. He felt the anger welling up inside. But then he remembered how he'd hit ALF with the ball. So he decided to try another way. He quickly began to move his arms about mechanically like a robot.

"Hello," he said in a robot like voice. "I'm Freddy, your friend in the box."

Michael and Alf doubled over, holding their
sides in laughter. Michael turned to Alf and said,
"We've been hunting in this jungle many times
before, but this is the first time we ever caught a
friend."

Then all three boys rolled with laughter on the
soft earth. It felt so good to laugh and
joke with friends. It felt good to
breathe the summer air and look up
through the green, shimmering leaves
to the shining sky. Freddy hadn't
felt this good for a long, long time.

A NEW FRIEND

B ack in The Hall of Harmoniousness, Heartly was brushing bits of tree bark from his fur. "A very tight squeeze," he murmured, remarking on their trip home.

"But worth it to help Freddy," yawned Heada as she stretched out on her bed.

"I'd do it again!" buzzed Doofer energetically. And he seemed ready to make the journey all over.

"No need for that," said a deep voice, and the three turned to see The Great Theysayer entering their room. "You all did your job very well."

ALF clanked mechanically across the floor and took the wise old man's hand.

"They say you did well, too, ALF," said The Great Theysayer, looking down at the little figure. "You gave Freddy a great gift."

"What?" asked ALF.

The Great Theysayer smiled. "The gift of making friends," he said. "They say it's a great gift for anyone."

A red, blushing color crept across ALF's video screen face, and he scuffed his little mechanical feet on the marble floor.

"Come along now," said The Great Theysayer. "I'll want your help again one day."

And with that, he led the little robot from the room.

"I like ALF," said Heartly wistfully, watching them go.

"Oh, Heartly!" cried Heada and Doofer together. "You like everybody!"

Heada's Dictionary
Words from the Tome

Accepts — *approves, believes*
Amends — *to make better; make up with a friend*
Brilliant — *bright; sparkling*
Diagrams — *designs that explain an idea*
   Energetically — *showing a great deal of action or energy*
   Exchanged nods — *traded nods of the head*
   Grimy — *dirty*
   Harmoniousness — *feelings, ideas, interests combined pleasantly*
Indescribably — *can not be described or explained*
Mission Accomplished — *the job is done*
Peculiarly peculiar — *very strange or odd*
Permanent — *something that lasts a long time*
Precisely — *exactly or correctly*
   Triumphantly — *being successful*
   Vanished — *gone from sight; disappeared*
Wistfully — *thoughtfully*

Other books from Family Skills:

School Age:

Self-Esteem: *Being a Friend to Myself*
Cooperation: *Working Together*
Feelings: *Dealing With Feelings*
Responsibility: *Making and Carrying Out a Plan*
Self-Talk: *Thinking and Feeling Good When Things Go Wrong*
Listening: *Giving and Getting Attention*
Friendship: *Keeping Friends*

Preschool:

Self-Esteem: *Adjusting to New Experience*
Responsibility: *Making and Living With Choices*
Feelings: *Experiencing Feelings*
Responsibility: *Understanding and Accepting Limits*
Self-Esteem: *Accepting and Knowing Myself*
Friendship: *Sharing and Taking Turns*